Duck Tour

Eagle

Fife

Isabella Stewart Gardner

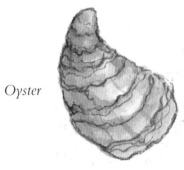
Juggler

Necco Wafer

Oyster

Puppet Showplace Theatre

Swan

Tory Row

Xmas Tree

Year 1630

MARTHA ZSCHOCK

Arboretum

Bottle

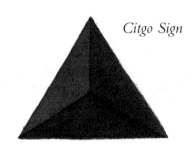

Citgo Sign

Gas Tank

Hub

Kelley

Lanterns

Magnolia

Quadrant

Red Sox

Union Park

Veterans

Walden Pond

Journey Around

Boston

from A to Z

by Martha Day Zschock

COMMONWEALTH EDITIONS

Beverly, Massachusetts

Commonwealth Editions
An Imprint of Memoirs Unlimited, Inc.
21 Lothrop Street
Beverly, MA 01915
Visit us at www.commonwealtheditions.com

ISBN 1-889833-19-3

10 9 8 7 6 5

Printed in Korea

To my wonderful family

and to all my frogpondian friends

*A special thank-you to those who have helped with this journey around Boston
and to the fact-checkers at the Boston National Historical Park,
especially park ranger Matt Greif.*

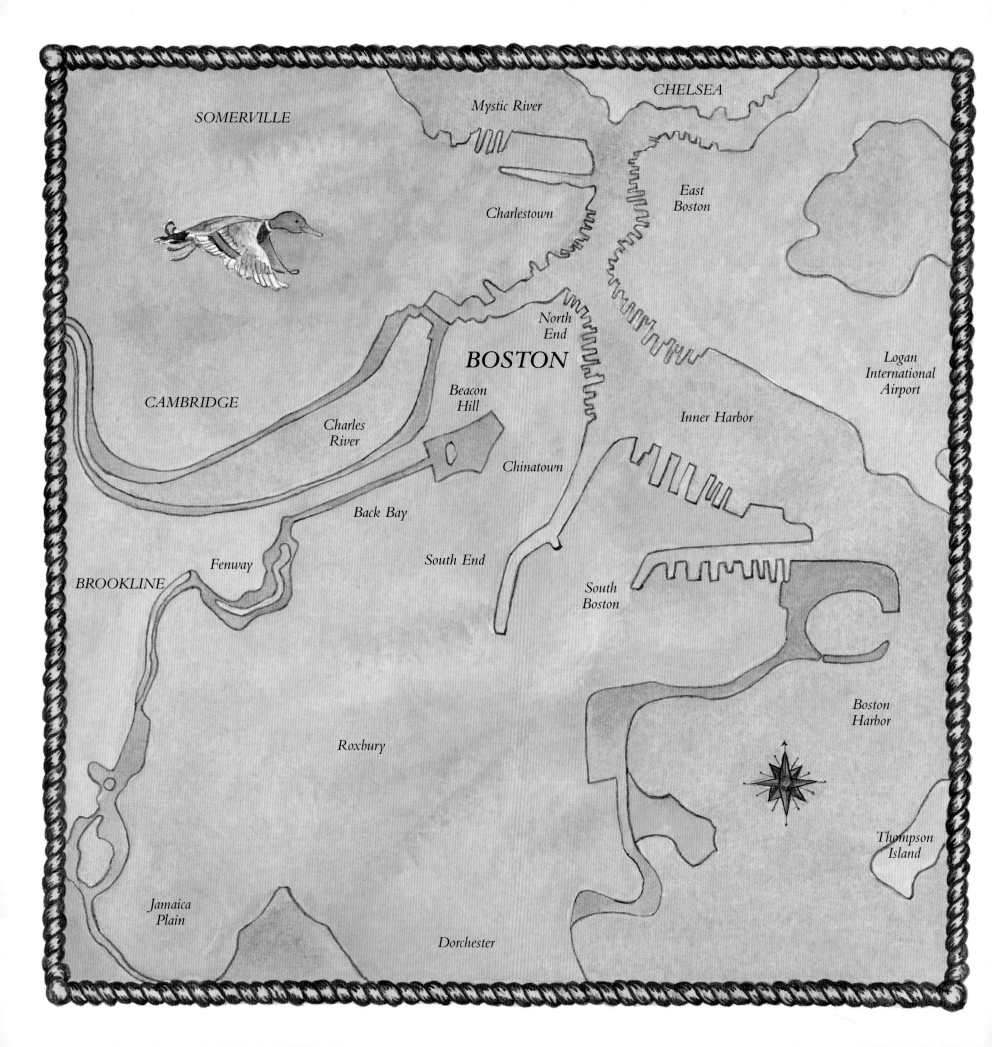

Welcome to Boston!

B EANTOWN, HUB OF THE SOLAR SYSTEM, Cradle of Liberty, Athens of America, City upon a Hill—Boston, by any name, is all of these and more.

Boston is a bustling city with strong ties to its past. When the Puritans first settled here in 1630, the area was a marshy peninsula called Shawmut. Native Americans visited to hunt and fish; the only year-round inhabitant was a hermit, Rev. William Blaxton. In building their colony, the Puritans laid the foundation of present-day Boston. They established schools, lowered hills, and filled in marshes. An aura of independence prevailed. Today, old and new meld together along Boston's notoriously crooked streets. From the faint scent of molasses in the North End to the graceful swan boats gliding in the Public Garden, from hoof prints embedded in a Cambridge sidewalk to headstones that don't always match the bones beneath them, Boston promises a story around every corner.

There is much to explore, so let's take a journey around Boston!

Let's hear it for the home team!

Abolitionists aided African-Americans.

COLONEL ROBERT GOULD SHAW led the first black regiment recruited in the North during the Civil War. A memorial to their bravery sits below Beacon Hill. In the early 1800s, many free African-Americans settled on Beacon Hill's north slope. Here stood the African Meeting House, where abolitionist William Lloyd Garrison formed the New England Anti-Slavery Society.

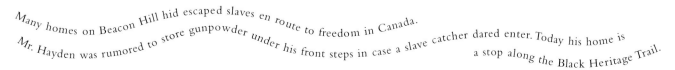

Many homes on Beacon Hill hid escaped slaves en route to freedom in Canada. Mr. Hayden was rumored to store gunpowder under his front steps in case a slave catcher dared enter. Today his home is a stop along the Black Heritage Trail.

Robert Gould Shaw Memorial, Boston Common
Insert: African Meeting House, Beacon Hill
Detail: Hayden House front steps, Beacon Hill

Brahmins built on Beacon Hill.

WITH ITS CHARMING BRICK BUILDINGS, cobblestone streets, gas lanterns, and lavender windowpanes, Beacon Hill became an "upper crust" neighborhood in the early 1800s after the new State House was built. Previously it was considered an undesirable area of cowpaths and brambles. It is named after the beacon once placed on its summit to signal for help in the event of an attack.

Beacon Hill, about sixty feet lower than it once was, is all that's left of the original three-peaked "Trimountain." The hills were excavated for use in landfill projects.

Lavender windowpanes, Beacon Hill
Insert: Old beacon
Detail: Trimountain

Chimes chorus in celebration.

TWO OF BOSTON'S MOST ELABORATE CHURCHES, Trinity Church and the Christian Science Church Center, are built on land that was once a stagnant marsh. By 1857, the "back bay" was so smelly that something had to be done. For over thirty years, countless loads of gravel were dumped into the marsh, transforming it into the neighborhood of Back Bay. Trinity Church sits on 4,500 pilings to keep it from sinking.

Arlington Street Church, the first church erected in Back Bay, has long been active in promoting freedom, peace, and equality.

Christian Science Church Center, Back Bay
Insert: Trinity Church, Back Bay
Detail: Arlington Street Church, Back Bay

Dumping dirt developed downtown.

KEY:
- Then
- Now

OVER THE YEARS Boston has been expanded and reshaped considerably by landfill projects. Wharves have pushed ever farther into the harbor. Since the Puritans first settled the peninsula in 1630, the area has grown dramatically. By adding land and other communities, Boston has become almost forty times its original size.

Boston's tallest buildings have a history of window problems. The Custom House Tower was once so close to the waterfront that boats bumped its windows. The John Hancock Tower had to replace all of its 10,344 panes after several popped out.

Downtown Boston, view from Cambridge
Insert: "Then and Now" map of Boston
Detail: John Hancock Tower, Prudential Center, and Custom House Tower

Education encourages excellence.

PEOPLE OF BOSTON established some of the country's first schools shortly after their arrival in the 1600s. Boston Latin School opened in 1635. A year later Harvard College began across the river in Cambridge with nine students and one teacher. Today there are about fifty colleges and universities within thirty miles of Boston.

Proper Boston children were once expected to be able to translate the Latin names posted on trees on Boston Common.

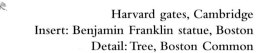

Harvard gates, Cambridge
Insert: Benjamin Franklin statue, Boston
Detail: Tree, Boston Common

Fans flock to Fenway.

FENWAY PARK is the smallest baseball stadium in the major leagues, and plans to build a new one are under way. The home of the Celtics (basketball) and Bruins (ice hockey) underwent a similar change from the old Boston Garden to the new Fleet Center in 1995. Fans hope the planned move will break the long-standing "Curse of the Bambino." The Red Sox have not won the World Series since Babe Ruth was sold to the New York Yankees over eighty years ago.

Fenway Park, The Fens
Insert: Statue of former Celtics coach Red Auerbach, Quincy Market
Details: Team jerseys: Bruins and Patriots

The Oneida Football Club (the country's first) played undefeated on Boston Common from 1862 to 1865. Now Boston's football team, the New England Patriots, play at Foxboro Stadium.

Glistening gold glorifies democracy's greatness.

THE "NEW" STATE HOUSE, designed by Charles Bulfinch, is actually over two hundred years old. The building cost $133,333.33, five times its original budget. Its 23-karat gilded dome was painted dark gray during World War II to keep its reflection in the moonlight from becoming an easy target for enemy bombers. Distances to other towns from Boston are calculated from the center of the dome.

A collection of flags from towns across Massachusetts hangs in the Great Hall of the State House.

State House Dome
Insert: Sacred Cod, House of Representatives, State House
Detail: Flags, Great Hall, State House

Honorable athletes hurry to Hancock.

ON PATRIOTS' DAY, the third Monday in April, tens of thousands of people gather to watch one of the world's most prestigious races, the Boston Marathon. The 26.2-mile run is the oldest annual marathon. Nearly ten thousand qualifiers and many unofficial participants start in Hopkinton and run through nine towns to the finish line near the John Hancock Tower in Copley Square.

Tortoise and Hare statue, Copley Square
Insert: Boston Marathon
Detail: Head of the Charles, Charles River

More than five thousand rowers from around the world compete in the Head of the Charles, another famous Boston race. Since racing shells start at different times, it's hard to tell who wins.

Invincible
Ironsides
remains intact.

USS *CONSTITUTION* earned its nickname, "Old Ironsides," while fighting the British warship HMS *Guerriere* in the War of 1812. Shots appeared to bounce off her strong wooden hull as if it had been made of iron. Launched in 1797, *Constitution* survived thirty-three engagements to become the world's oldest commissioned warship afloat and the oldest sailing ship still able to sail under her own power.

Bunker Hill Monument, which actually sits on Breed's Hill, watches over Charlestown Navy Yard and the fancy Commandant's House. At 221 feet, it is one foot taller than "Old Ironsides'" mainmast.

"Old Ironsides," Charlestown Navy Yard
Insert: Bunker Hill Monument, Charlestown
Detail: Commandant's House, Charlestown Navy Yard

Jolly times are had at July jamborees.

ARTHUR FIEDLER, conductor of the Boston Pops from 1930 to 1979, believed that music is for everyone: old, young, rich, and poor. Each July, he moved his orchestra from their home at Symphony Hall to the Hatch Shell on the banks of the Charles River to give a series of free concerts, a tradition that continues each summer.

Symphony Hall is almost perfect acoustically. It's said that from the center of the second balcony you can hear a pin drop on stage.

Hatch Shell, The Esplanade
Insert: Arthur Fiedler statue, The Esplanade
Detail: Symphony Hall, Back Bay

Kennedy led with courage and kindness.

JOHN F. KENNEDY served as our thirty-fifth president for 1,036 days until he was shot and killed in Dallas, Texas, on November 22, 1963. An intelligent, courageous, and optimistic leader, he inspired hope in the American people. He believed that one person can make a difference and everyone should try. The Kennedy Library and Museum is a tribute to his greatness.

A pretty rose garden dedicated to JFK's mother, Rose Kennedy, blooms on the edge of the North End, where she was born.

Flag, John F. Kennedy Library and Museum
Insert: John F. Kennedy statue, State House
Detail: Rose Kennedy Rose Garden, North End

Lions live in the library lobby.

IN CELEBRATION OF THEIR LOVE FOR LEARNING, Bostonians built their library as a "Palace for the People" in 1895, making it "free to all." The most famous artists and architects of the day worked on its creation, which became a model for the rest of the country. The Boston Public Library was the first in the country with a room just for children.

Marble lions, Boston Public Library
Insert: Children's room, BPL
Detail: Longfellow House, Cambridge

Among poet Henry Wadsworth Longfellow's many works are *The Song of Hiawatha* and *Paul Revere's Ride.*

ON THE EVENING OF APRIL 18, 1775, British redcoats marched toward Lexington and Concord to seize weapons and ammunition stored by rebellious colonists. The local militia, the "minutemen," had been warned and were prepared to fight. The next morning, "the shot heard 'round the world" rang out from the battles at Lexington and Concord, marking the beginning of the Revolutionary War.

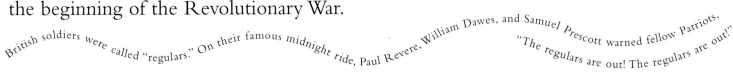

British soldiers were called "regulars." On their famous midnight ride, Paul Revere, William Dawes, and Samuel Prescott warned fellow Patriots, "The regulars are out! The regulars are out!"

Minuteman statue, Lexington
Insert: Old North Bridge, Concord
Detail: Duck riding on horse

Neighbor-hoods nurtured new arrivals.

IMMIGRANTS FLOCKED TO BOSTON for a variety of reasons and settled in ethnic neighborhoods. Many Irish, escaping potato famine in their homeland, eventually settled in South Boston. Chinatown became home to many Chinese who found work laying lines for the quickly expanding phone company. Many Italians chose the North End. Today the neighborhoods have become more diverse, but still maintain their ethnic flavor.

Irish Immigrant statue, downtown
Insert: Gates, Chinatown
Detail: Religious festival, North End

The North End, like many ethnic neighborhoods, hosts street celebrations and festivals.

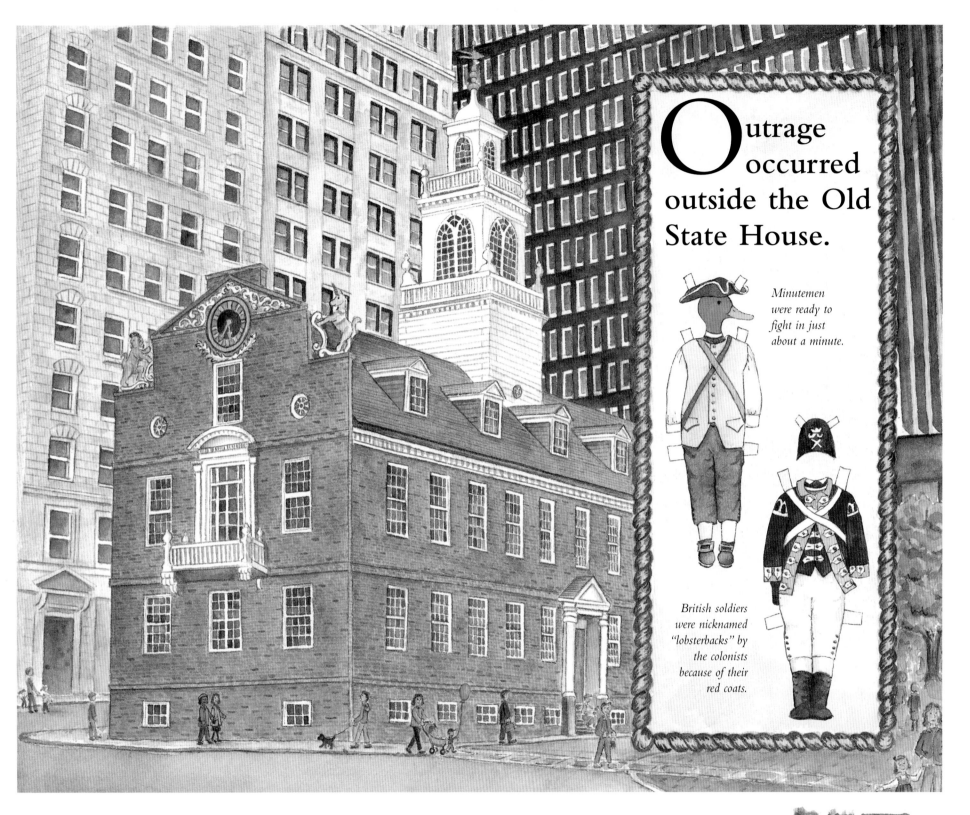

Outrage **o**ccurred outside the Old State House.

Minutemen were ready to fight in just about a minute.

British soldiers were nicknamed "lobsterbacks" by the colonists because of their red coats.

SHORT OF MONEY after a war with France in the mid-1700s, Britain placed a tax on many goods sold to the colonies. This angered colonists who felt it was unfair. British troops were sent to keep order, but this only made matters worse. On March 5, 1770, snowballs, rocks, and taunting triggered the Boston Massacre. Five colonists were killed and many others were hurt during the skirmish.

A cobblestone marker in the ground near the Old State House is close to the spot of the Boston Massacre.

Old State House, downtown
Insert: Costumes of minutemen and redcoats
Detail: Boston Massacre marker, downtown

Parks are preserved for peaceful pastimes.

Public Garden

Back Bay Fens

Muddy River Improvement

Olmsted Park

Jamaica Pond

Franklin Park

Arnold Arboretum

THE BOSTON PUBLIC GARDEN is known for its swan boats, duckling statues, and a miniature bridge that once may have been the world's smallest suspension bridge. It marks the beginning of the Emerald Necklace, a chain of parks that laces its way through Boston to the Franklin Park Zoo in Dorchester. The chain, designed by landscape architect Frederick Law Olmsted, creates a "countryish escape in the midst of city life."

Make Way for Ducklings.

 In order to make his pictures realistic, author-illustrator Robert McCloskey kept ten mallard ducks in his New York City apartment while working on

Swan Boat, Boston Public Garden
Insert: Map of the Emerald Necklace
Detail: Duckling statues, Boston Public Garden

Quaint carts line Quincy Market.

EVERY TRUE BOSTONIAN knows that a gilded copper grasshopper weathervane watches over Faneuil Hall, a public market and meeting site. Just in front of it sits Quincy Market which once housed meat and produce distributors. In the 1970s, the area was festively renovated and now has many quaint shops, specialty carts, and tasty treats.

Nearby, the Haymarket bustles with vendors selling fruits and vegetables every Friday and Saturday.

Quincy Market, downtown
Insert: Grasshopper weathervane, Faneuil Hall
Detail: Haymarket, downtown

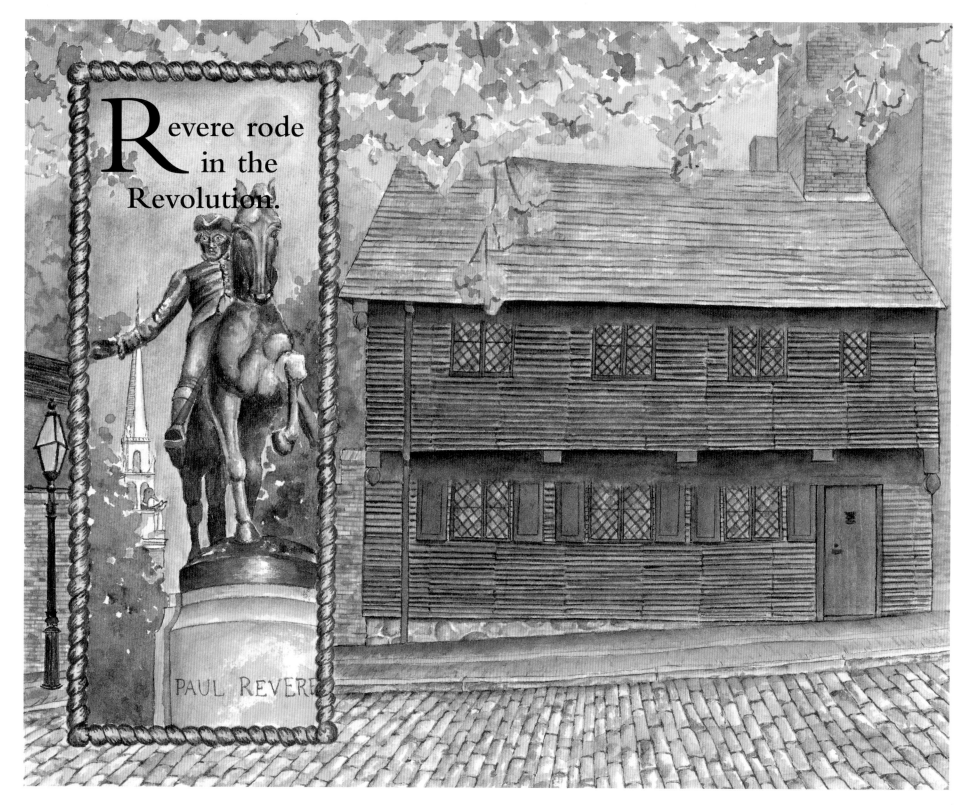

Revere rode in the Revolution.

PAUL REVERE'S FAMOUS MIDNIGHT RIDE was only one of his many accomplishments. He was a silversmith, an engraver, and a dentist; he made the first church bell cast in Boston and rolled copper for the bottoms of warships like "Old Ironsides" and for the dome of the new State House. He was also the father of sixteen children!

Paul Revere's largest bell weighed 2,437 pounds. He wouldn't consider a sale final until his customer was pleased with the bell's tone.

Paul Revere House, North End
Insert: Paul Revere statue and Old North Church, North End
Detail: Revere Bell

Sun shines on solemn sadness.

MARY DYER

QUAKER

ETCHED IN THE GLASS TOWERS of the New England Holocaust Memorial are six million numbers representing the Jewish victims of Nazi death camps. Outside the State House stands a statue of Mary Dyer, who was hanged for upholding her Quaker beliefs. These memorials, and many others in and around Boston, are solemn reminders that freedom and respect for human rights are cornerstones of American belief.

In dedicating the Salem Witch Trials Memorial, Holocaust survivor Elie Wiesel found many similarities to other historical horrors.

Holocaust Memorial, downtown
Insert: Statue of Mary Dyer, State House
Detail: Salem Witch Trials Memorial, Salem

Too many taxes tipped the tea.

AFTER THE BOSTON MASSACRE, the British lifted all taxes except that on tea. Colonists were not satisfied. After three British ships loaded with tea docked at the wharf, Bostonians debated what to do. Thousands rallied at the Old South Meeting House on December 16, 1773. Afterward, a group of men and boys dressed as American Indians boarded the British ships and dumped 342 chests of tea into the harbor.

A guessing contest in 1875 determined that one of Boston's favorite signs, the "steaming tea kettle," could hold 227 gallons, two quarts, one pint, and three gills of tea.

Tea Party Ship, waterfront
Insert: Old South Meeting House, downtown
Detail: Steaming Tea Kettle, downtown

Under and over the urban landscape.

THE FIRST SUBWAY

PARK

Airport Exit ↗
B C E
Departures ↗ ↗

BY THE LATE 1800S, Boston's narrow streets were so crowded with trolley cars that the decision was made to go underground. The city built the first U.S. subway, now known as the T. Today, the huge Central Artery Tunnel Project, or the Big Dig, again hopes to solve Boston's traffic problems by burying them. Traffic controllers at Logan International Airport orchestrate approximately six hundred takeoffs and six hundred landings each day.

With its ever-rising costs, the Big Dig is one of the most expensive public works projects in U.S. history.

Mural, Park Street Station
Insert: Logan International Airport
Detail: The Big Dig

Visitors
venture to
a variety of
views.

BOSTON COMMON began as a common grazing ground for cattle. It was also used for military training, hangings, public speeches, and just plain fun. The well-traveled Freedom Trail begins here at the Visitor Center. Following a red brick line, folks visit sixteen key sites along this country's journey to independence.

Visitor Center, Boston Common
Insert: Freedom Trail Map
Details: Frog Pond, Boston Common

The Common's Frog Pond no longer contains frogs but is fun to splash in during the summer and skate on in the winter.

PERCHED ON TOP OF LITTLE BREWSTER ISLAND, Boston Light was America's first lighthouse. Its beacon, which can be seen twenty-seven miles out to sea, warns sailors of the thirty islands that dot Boston Harbor. A beacon atop the old John Hancock Building forecasts the weather: solid blue, clear view; flashing blue, clouds due; solid red, rain ahead; flashing red, snow instead. In summer flashing red warns fans that the Red Sox are rained out.

Boston's Harbor Islands, which have held forts, a children's hospital, prisons, and illegal gambling houses, are now mostly protected as a National Recreation Area.

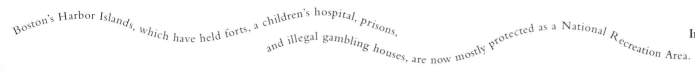

Boston Light, Little Brewster Island
Insert: Old John Hancock Building, Back Bay
Detail: Boston Harbor Islands

E**X**traordinary
exhibits
excite viewers.

NOT ALL MUSEUMS are simply for viewing. The Museum of Science and the Children's Museum encourage kids to use their hands to explore and discover. The display of three thousand blown-glass flowers at Harvard's Botanical Museum and the Egyptian mummies at the Boston Museum of Fine Arts are worth a visit even though you can't touch them.

From bubbles to dinosaurs, from life-size computers to larger-than-life paintings, kids will never be bored in Boston's museums!

Kinetic Sculpture, Museum of Science
Insert: Blaschka Glass Flowers, Harvard's Botanical Museum
Details: Scenes from Boston museums

Yarns have been spun at Ye Olde Union Oyster House for years.

BOSTON IS OFTEN REFERRED TO as "Beantown" or "home of the bean and the cod." Baked beans sweetened with molasses have been a local favorite since Puritan days, when no cooking could be done on Sunday. Beans were prepared on Saturday and left to simmer until dinner the following day. Baked beans and cod are still popular at Boston's oldest restaurant, the Union Oyster House.

Although lobster is a delicacy today, colonists thought it was fit only for prisoners, servants, and the poor.

Union Oyster House, downtown
Insert: Boston Baked Beans and Boston Cream Pie
Detail: Lobster

Zoodopters adopt zoo animals.

 THE FRANKLIN PARK ZOO and the New England Aquarium exhibit animals in their natural habitats. The aquarium has an enormous four-story ocean-reef tank, and an exhibit at the zoo recreates the environment of the Australian outback. The aquarium is well known for helping marine animals that become stranded or caught in nets. Both organizations have programs that let kids "adopt" unusual animals like flamingos, gorillas, and whales.

The Freedom Trail has a zoo of its own. Look for a glass-eyed grasshopper, a wooden lion and a unicorn, an eagle, and a black metal cow.

Lion's den, Franklin Park Zoo
Insert: Penguin Tank, New England Aquarium
Details: Animals found on the Freedom Trail

 *Duck Tour*

 *Eagle*

 *Fife*

 *Isabella Stewart Gardner*

 *Juggler*

 *Necco Wafer*

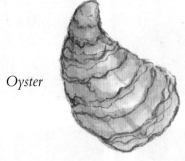 *Oyster*

 *Puppet Showplace Theatre*

 *Swan*

 *Tory Row*

 *Xmas Tree*

 *Year 1630*

Arboretum

Bottle

Citgo Sign

Gas Tank

Hub

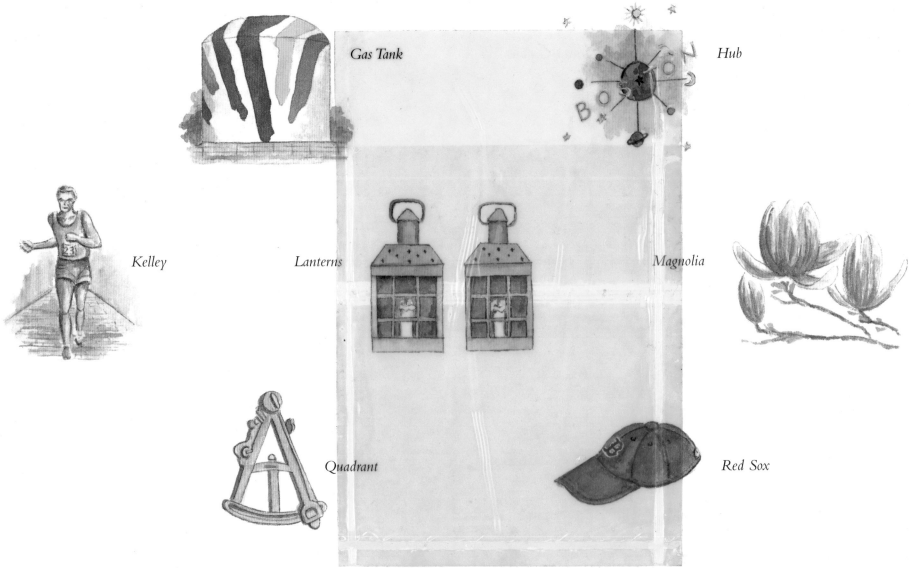

Kelley

Lanterns

Magnolia

Quadrant

Red Sox

Union Park

Veterans

Walden Pond